CW00750400

John Knox

by Simonetta Carr

with Illustrations by Matt Abraxas

REFORMATION HERITAGE BOOKS
Grand Rapids, Michigan

John Knox
© 2014 by Simonetta Carr

Cover artwork by Matt Abraxas: Knox leaves England for nearby France.

For additional artwork by Matt, see pages 9, 13, 17, 21, 23, 29, 31, 33, 39, 43, 47, 53, 55.

All rights reserved. No part of this book may be used or reproduced in any manner whatsoever without written permission except in the case of brief quotations embodied in critical articles and reviews. Direct your requests to the publisher at the following address:

Reformation Heritage Books
2965 Leonard St. NE
Grand Rapids, MI 49525
616-977-0889 / Fax: 616-285-3246
e-mail: orders@heritagebooks.org
website: www.heritagebooks.org

Printed in the United States of America
14 15 16 17 18 19/10 9 8 7 6 5 4 3 2 1

Library of Congress Cataloging-in-Publication Data

Carr, Simonetta.
  John Knox / by Simonetta Carr ; with illustrations by Matt Abraxas.
    pages cm. — (Christian biographies for young readers)
  ISBN 978-1-60178-289-2 (hardcover : alk. paper) 1. Knox, John, approximately 1514-1572—Juvenile literature. 2. Reformation—Scotland—Biography—Juvenile literature. I. Abraxas, Matt, illustrator. II. Title.
  BX9223.C37 2014
  285'.2092—dc23
  [B]
                                        2013042509

For additional Reformed literature, request a free book list from Reformation Heritage Books at the above address.

CHRISTIAN BIOGRAPHIES FOR YOUNG READERS

This series introduces children to important people in the Christian tradition. Parents and schoolteachers alike will welcome the excellent educational value it provides for students, while the quality of the publication and the artwork make each volume a keepsake for generations to come. Furthermore, the books in the series go beyond the simple story of someone's life by teaching young readers the historical and theological relevance of each character.

AVAILABLE VOLUMES OF THE SERIES
John Calvin
Augustine of Hippo
John Owen
Athanasius
Lady Jane Grey
Anselm of Canterbury
John Knox

SOME ANTICIPATED VOLUMES
Jonathan Edwards
Julia Gonzaga
Martin Luther
…and more

Table of Contents

MAP CREATED BY TOM CARROLL

A map of Western Europe during John Knox's life. You may want to use it to follow his travels.

Introduction

As a schoolboy growing up in the small Scottish town of Haddington, John Knox could never have imagined that he would become a major leader of a powerful movement that would transform Scotland into one of the most committed Protestant countries in the world.

OLD EDINBURGH, ACTUAL EDUCATION LTD.

John Knox, as he was portrayed in a book published around his time.

Around the time Knox was born, probably in 1514, Scotland was a small, remote country that many people considered wild and mysterious. Still, even in that faraway corner of the world, as in most of Europe, people had started to voice their disappointment in the leaders of the Roman Catholic Church, which was the only type of Christian church in Western Europe. Some of the problems were obvious: these leaders often became rich at the expense of the poor or defiantly broke God's commandments to satisfy their selfish desires. Some people, however, protested against deeper problems: they believed some of the church's teachings were contrary to the Bible. These protestors were later called Protestants.

© THE HUNTERIAN, UNIVERSITY OF GLASGOW 2013

PATRICIUS
HAMILTON

Cranlodi Mart
Panatus Fob 15?

This is the only portrait of Patrick Hamilton. It was painted more than a hundred years after his death, so we can't be absolutely sure the Reformer looked like this.

At first, most Protestants lived in Germany and Switzerland, and Scottish Roman Catholic authorities tried hard to keep books and ideas from those countries out of Scotland. They also tried to keep the common people from reading the Bible. If everyone read it, they thought, there would be too many interpretations and a lot of confusion.

Some Scots, however, traveled to other countries, where they discovered the gospel as exciting, good news: Christ did everything for our salvation, and the special offerings, good works, and prayers the church was requiring were not necessary to earn it. One of these Scottish travelers was Patrick Hamilton, who heard the gospel in France and then spread the news in Scotland until he was captured and killed. The authorities hoped his death would stop others from embracing his beliefs. Instead, many who had never thought about these matters began wondering why he had been killed and if maybe he had been right.

CHAPTER ONE
A Young Man in a Troubled Country

Hailes Castle, near Haddington. It seems that Knox's grandfathers and father provided some service to the castle owners, the Earls of Bothwell.

John Knox was about fifteen at the time of Hamilton's death, and he probably heard about it because Hamilton was the first Protestant in Scotland to die for his faith. We don't know anything about Knox's childhood, but at this time he might have enrolled at St. Andrews University—or he may have been getting ready to go there—because young people then started university much earlier than they do now.

After Knox finished his studies, he was ordained to be a priest, but he used his knowledge of church law mainly to work as a notary in and around Haddington. Notaries usually check documents and sign them to show that what is written in them is correct. It was probably a fairly quiet job.

In the meantime, many things in Scotland were changing. The king, James V, died from a sudden illness, leaving the throne to his six-day-old daughter, Mary Stuart. Because she was only a baby, the Earl of Arran (we will call him Arran from now on) was chosen to make decisions for her. Eager to make peace with England, a long-time enemy of Scotland, Arran discussed with its king, Henry VIII, the idea of a future marriage between Mary and Henry's son, Edward, who was five at that time.

Portrait of James Hamilton, 2nd Earl of Arran and Duke of Chatelherault, by Arnold Van Bronckhorst

IN THE COLLECTION OF LENNOXLOVE HOUSE LIMITED, HADDINGTON © 2013. REPRODUCED BY KIND PERMISSION BY HIS GRACE THE DUKE OF HAMILTON.

King Henry had broken all ties with the Church of Rome. With the backing of this powerful friend, Arran decided to allow some freedom of worship to the Protestant lords who had been requesting it. For the first time, the common people were allowed to read the Bible. During this time Knox heard God's message of salvation through faith alone preached in a church. The sermon might have been on John 17, because later Knox said that chapter is where he cast his "first anchor."

Knox heard the preaching of God's message of salvation through faith alone in Christ.

King Henry VIII

WWW.HERITAGE-HISTORY.COM

Around the same time, Knox became a tutor for three boys from two families, teaching them typical subjects such as Latin grammar and literature, English, and possibly French. Because they were Protestant, the boys also studied the Bible. Knox probably enjoyed this time of freedom.

This freedom and peace, however, didn't last long. King Henry started to make strong demands on Scotland, so the Scottish leaders tossed out any idea of giving Mary to his son in marriage. Furious, Henry sent a large army to terrorize the people, and the soldiers burned whole cities, including the area where Knox lived. He even sent men to kidnap Mary, but the Scottish leaders hid her well.

At that point, most of the Scottish leaders looked for help from France, where Mary Stuart's mother, Mary of Guise, was born. Arran sided with these leaders. Since France was a Roman Catholic country, he put a stop to the freedom the Protestants had been given.

CHAPTER TWO
From Bodyguard to Preacher

Even though Protestants were no longer free, some continued to proclaim the gospel around the country. George Wishart was an important preacher who had studied the Protestant teachings in England and Switzerland and proclaimed them boldly both in churches and open-air sermons. He had a band of close followers who went with him to assist and protect him. These followers included Knox and the two men who had hired Knox as a tutor. At this time, both Wishart and Knox were about thirty years old. Preaching in public was dangerous, and Wishart knew that one day he would be killed. Still, he said he would always dare to preach if people dared to listen.

George Wishart.
We can't be sure he
looked like this.

After a while it was clear that Wishart would not be able to avoid the authorities who were trying to catch him. Knox and his friends wanted to stay with him until the end, but Wishart sent them home, saying, "No, return to your boys, and God bless you. One is sufficient for a sacrifice."

Probably Knox had mixed feelings. He loved Wishart very much and wanted to fight for the gospel until the end, but he understood that sometimes it's better to stay alive and fight other battles. He said good-bye to his dear friend, gave up the sword, and returned home with his students' fathers.

That same night, at midnight, some guards surrounded the house where Wishart was staying. At first they offered to protect him if he surrendered, but when he did, they took him to Cardinal David Beaton, the highest authority in the Roman Catholic Church in Scotland, who imprisoned him as a rebel.

Wishart asked Knox to give up his sword.

On March 1, 1546, Wishart was put to death. Knox mourned him as "a man of such graces as before him were never heard within this realm, and are rare to be found yet in any man." Like Knox, most Protestants quietly lamented his death. Some, however, decided to do more. On May 29, eighteen men forcibly entered the castle at St. Andrews, where Cardinal Beaton lived. They killed the cardinal in his bedroom and hung his body on the castle wall for all to see. They had planned this attack for a long time. Then they took possession of the castle. Soon, others joined them, until the castle became an actual Protestant fortress.

OLD EDINBURGH IMAGES, ACTUAL EDUCATION LTD.

Cardinal David Beaton

Fearing that the government would fight back, Knox moved from home to home to stay safe. He even thought of leaving the country. Finally, in April 1547, his students' fathers suggested that he move, with their sons, to St. Andrews Castle, and Knox agreed.

BILL MCKENZIE/BMPHOTO

St. Andrews Castle. It was hard to conquer from land but easier from the water. On the left of the castle you can see St. Andrews Church, where Knox preached his first sermon.

Knox found safety at St. Andrews, partially because the castle was fortified, difficult to conquer by land, and protected by armed Protestants. Also, the Protestants were keeping Arran's son hostage there, so for a long time there were no attacks. In fact, the Protestants who lived there were free to go in and out as they pleased.

Every day Knox took his students to the chapel at St. Andrews Castle, where he read and explained to them the gospel of John. Two men watched him with great interest: Henry Balnaves and John Rough. They had worked hard for years to persuade the government to allow English Bibles and the free preaching of the gospel in Scotland. These men encouraged Knox to preach at the local church on Sunday. The situation at this church may seem strange to us, because Protestant and Roman Catholic ministers took turns preaching and explaining their views.

Knox didn't think God had called him to be a preacher, but he agreed to help Rough prepare a speech explaining why some teachings of the Roman Catholic Church were wrong. The speech was so clear and convincing that Rough was sure that Knox should preach. The following Sunday, in his sermon, Rough explained that the members of the church had the authority to choose their pastor. He then repeated with great passion his invitation to Knox, pleading with him to accept it for the glory of God and the good of Christ's kingdom. When he asked the people if they agreed, everyone said yes. Overwhelmed, Knox burst into tears and had to retire to his room.

Overwhelmed by an invitation to pastor a church, Knox burst into tears and had to retire to his room.

During the next week, Knox stayed in his room most of the time, praying and thinking. Becoming a preacher and a pastor was a great responsibility. The next Sunday, he went back to church for worship. There, the Catholic priest explained that the Church of Rome had the final say because it was the bride of Christ. Knox stood up to voice his disagreement: the Church of Rome was no longer Christ's bride because it had left His teachings, and Knox believed he could prove it. The people appreciated his convictions and asked him to preach the following Sunday. Knox believed that the people's invitation was a confirmation of God's calling. The next Sunday, he rose to the pulpit to preach for the first time.

In his sermon, Knox explained that Christ is the only Head of the church, and only the Bible has the final say. He also showed how many of the traditions of the Roman Catholic Church had been invented by men. His words left a great impression on the people. They felt he was getting to the root of the problems. Some were worried about him and said, "Master George Wishart never spoke so openly, and yet he was burnt. Even so will John Knox be."

CHAPTER THREE
Hard Labor and Chains

The government of Scotland continued to make plans to recapture St. Andrews Castle. The Scottish leaders were especially afraid that England might side with the Protestants and use the castle to conquer the rest of the country. Finally, they asked the French government for help. In June 1547, a French fleet of warships arrived. It was easier to attack the castle from the water, and the French soon captured it.

The French arrested all the Protestants at St. Andrews. Those who were considered most important, including the men who had killed Cardinal Beaton, were imprisoned, and the rest, including Knox, were sent to the galleys. Galleys were ships that were used during wars. They had sails, but if the wind dropped, about 150 slaves, chained to the benches, were forced to row for many hours.

WWW.HERITAGE-HISTORY.COM

Galleys at war

Life on galleys was so hard that some prisoners confessed to crimes they never committed because they would rather be killed than row on a galley. Many died from overwork and disease. Sometimes galleys sank in rough seas or were bombarded or burned during wars, and the chained prisoners had no way to save themselves. Years later, in his book about the history of the Reformation in Scotland, Knox mentioned this experience, explaining that galley slaves were "miserably treated."

Sometimes, the galleys' Roman Catholic supervisors tried to force the slaves to pray to Mary, the mother of Jesus, but Knox and other Protestants refused. They believed the Bible teaches us to pray to God alone, and praying to anything or anyone else is idolatry, a very serious sin. Knox wrote that once the supervisors pushed a painting of Mary against a prisoner's face to force him to kiss it, but the prisoner threw it overboard, saying, "Let our Lady now save herself!" Even though Knox described what happened with the painting as though he were writing about another person, he was probably the man who refused to kiss the painting. Knox didn't write much about this time of his life, but he thought this story was important because he always fought hard against any form of idolatry.

Refusing to kiss a painting of Mary, a prisoner—probably Knox—threw it overboard.

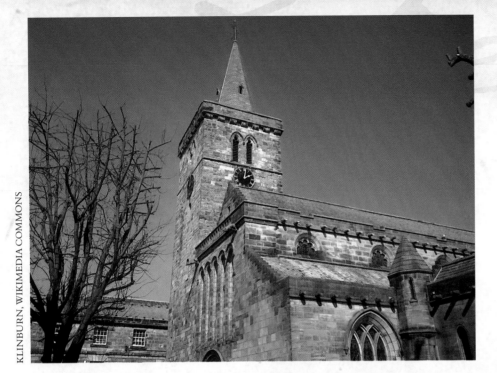

KLINBURN, WIKIMEDIA COMMONS

The Tower of Holy Trinity Parish Church, where John Knox preached his first sermon.

Once winter was over, Knox continued to row while the French fought the English along the coasts of Scotland, his country. It must have been difficult for him to pass by the places where he had played as a child and worked as a young man, knowing the war he was helping to fight was bringing much suffering to his countrymen.

During a war, the prisoners had to row faster than ever. The normal diet of biscuits and water, with a vegetable soup three times a week, was not enough to keep them strong and healthy. As they got close to St. Andrews, Knox became so sick that everyone thought he was going to die. Then the man next to him, who had also been with him at St. Andrews, told him to look at the land. Knox was chained to the bench, and the side of the galley was six feet high, but with some difficulty he managed to see the tower of the church where he had preached his first sermon. Suddenly, he knew he would preach there again and found strength to keep living.

Seeing the steeple of St. Andrews Church, where he had preached his first sermon, Knox found strength to keep living.

During the winter months, the galleys didn't sail, and the prisoners spent much of their time making mats, blankets, and other objects to sell so they could buy extra food. Knox, however, had just received a book his friend Henry Balnaves had written. He was imprisoned in a castle nearby, and he had asked Knox to revise his book. Knox found great comfort in the book and worked hard at revising it, dividing it into chapters and adding a short summary for quick review.

The main question of the book was this: What should we do in time of trouble? The answer was we should go directly to God in prayer, running to Him as a wild deer runs to the river in the burning heat of the day, and expect salvation only from Him without trusting in good works, images, saints, holy water, or anything else. It also explained that our eternal salvation, which is the most important thing, is only by God's grace and only through faith in Christ. The officers in the galleys must have thought Knox was foolish to spend his time writing instead of making money, but they didn't care as long as Knox could still row.

The Tower of Rouen,
a portion of the castle where
Henry Balnaves was held prisoner.

EDHRAL, WIKIMEDIA COMMONS

CHAPTER FOUR
A New Home in England

To Knox's surprise, at the beginning of 1549, nineteen months after his capture, the French government freed him and some other slaves, probably because of some kind of prisoners' exchange with England, where twelve-year-old Edward VI was on the throne. Edward was a convinced Protestant and was glad to have a fiery preacher like Knox in his country.

Trying to find the best place for Knox in England, Edward's Royal Council sent him to the small town of Berwick, only three miles from the Scottish border. Most of the English people, especially in faraway places like Berwick, knew little about the Bible, so Knox had a big job to do. He also spent some time preaching in nearby Newcastle. Many Scots lived in that area, and some came from Scotland just to hear him preach.

King Edward VI
OLD EDINBURGH IMAGES, ACTUAL EDUCATION LTD.

Since Berwick and Newcastle were border towns, they had a large population of soldiers—rough men who were often ready to pick a fight. As they heard the message of Christ's free salvation for sinners, however, their behavior improved, and there was less violence. While there, Knox wrote a short book to teach the people in his church how to pray, assuring them that even when everything seems to go wrong, God is faithful to His people.

It was around this time that Knox met Marjory Bowes, a young woman who later became his wife. Marjory and her mother, Elizabeth, were eager students of the Bible and loved to listen to the preaching of the gospel. Marjory's father, Robert, was stationed as captain at Norham Castle, where Knox preached a few times.

ADRIAN NICHOLLS

Norham Castle, home of the Bowes family.
From there, Knox would have seen Scotland easily.

In the autumn of 1551, Knox accepted an invitation to move to London to be one of the king's preachers. While he was there, he continued to correspond with Marjory and her mother, encouraging them to trust God. Mrs. Bowes had many questions about the Bible and

A preacher named Hugh Latimer preaches to Edward VI, and this may be how John Knox preached too. At that time, people were often standing during sermons. The engraving is from John Foxe's *Acts and Monuments*.

salvation. She asked, for example, "Can God continue to forgive us even if we never seem to do better?" Knox knew well the weight of his own sins. "I am worse than my pen can express," he said. On the other hand, he knew and believed God's promises to forgive him.

"Don't despair, Mother," he wrote to her once. "God can forgive all your sins, even if you had committed thousands of them. What? Do you think that God's goodness, mercy, and grace can be overcome by your iniquities? Will God, who cannot undo His work of salvation, be a liar, and lose His own glory, because you are a sinner?" Both Knox and Mrs. Bowes knew the answer was no. God cannot lie, and our sins are not greater than His grace.

Being a royal preacher was a great honor that allowed Knox to share some of his concerns and fears about England with the king. He thought the Church of England was still too close to the traditions of the Roman Catholic Church and ran the risk of inspiring idolatry instead of pure worship of God. He also noticed that some of the king's councillors cared for their own interests more than the good of the country. To him, these things represented a serious danger for both the church and the country.

His fears became reality on July 6, 1553, when, following an unexpected illness, King Edward died, and his half-sister Mary Tudor, a Roman Catholic, was proclaimed queen. Soon, she imposed her religion on her subjects. Protestants were left with the choice of leaving England or dying for their faith. After a few months of hiding, Knox made the difficult decision to leave and traveled by boat to nearby France. As much as he loved his native country, he said the troubles in England were at that point twice as painful to his heart "as ever were the troubles in Scotland."

After a few months of hiding, Knox made the difficult decision to leave England and crossed the English Channel to nearby France.

29

Henry Bullinger
WWW.REFORMATIONART.COM

CHAPTER FIVE
A School of Christ

John Calvin
WWW.REFORMATIONART.COM

After a short stay in France, Knox traveled to Switzerland, where he visited two famous Reformers: John Calvin in Geneva and Henry Bullinger in Zurich. He learned a great deal just from watching their lives and the way their churches worshiped and worked. In fact, he admired the way Geneva was run so much that he called it "the most perfect school of Christ that was ever on earth since the days of the apostles." He also took this time to ask the Reformers some questions that had lain heavily on his mind: May a young boy such as Edward rule a country? May women rule? And if a ruler such as Mary Tudor demands that the people disobey God's Word, are they allowed to rebel?

The Reformers reminded Knox that the Bible teaches us to obey those who have authority over us, even if we don't agree with them, unless they ask us to do something contrary to God's Word. In that case, we can leave the country, or we can disobey and suffer the consequences. Rebellion can be a possibility in some cases, but Calvin and Bullinger advised Knox to be careful because sometimes people use their religion as an excuse to rebel. Knox followed their advice but kept thinking about this for a long time.

In 1555, Knox returned to Scotland and to Berwick briefly to see Marjory again. It was around that time that he and Marjory got married. Then Marjory and her mother made plans to move to Geneva with him.

Knox's enemies in Scotland made a huge puppet that looked like him and burned it publicly.

Knox was astonished to see how many people in Scotland had become passionate for the gospel, risking their lives to worship together in private homes. For about nine months, he preached in many towns to enthusiastic audiences. When the Catholic leaders heard about his preaching, they called Knox to be tried in their court of law, but he had so many supporters that they quickly dropped their plans. Later, they decided to call him again, but by that time he had already left for Geneva. Finally, they made a huge puppet that looked like him and burned it publicly. Maybe they wanted to warn the people not to follow his example. In reality, they made him only more famous.

A page of the 1560 Geneva Bible, one of the first English translations of the Bible from the original Hebrew and Greek. Several members of John Knox's church in Geneva contributed to this translation.

In Geneva, Knox became pastor of a church of English people who had fled from England to escape Mary Tudor. These people were eager to hear the gospel and obey God's Word. They organized the church and its worship according to the New Testament. Knox worked together with another pastor, the English Christopher Goodman, who became one of his best friends for life.

Marjory and her mother also joined him in Geneva. Within the first few years of marriage, he and Marjory had two sons, Nathaniel and Eleazar. Besides being a busy mother, Marjory helped Knox write letters and organize his papers. She was also a caring hostess, ready to open her home to many of the visitors who stayed in Geneva. Knox found much comfort in his marriage. He called Marjory "my left hand" and "that which of earthly creatures is most dear to me."

As most Reformers, John Knox led his family in worship every day. Their home was often full of visitors.

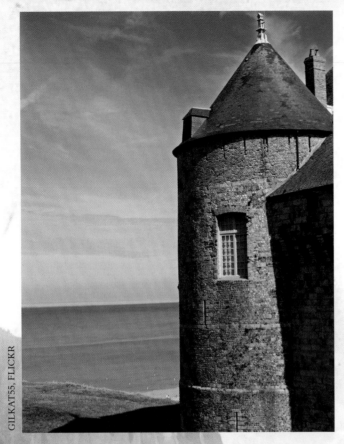

GILKAT55, FLICKR

The medieval castle of Dieppe, overlooking the waters of the English Channel. Knox may have looked longingly to the other side of the sea as he waited for a permit to land in England.

This was probably the happiest time in Knox's life. At the same time, he didn't forget his friends in Scotland and wrote to them often. They invited him to return, but things didn't work out for a while. Calvin, however, kept encouraging him to go back, because most of the people who came to Geneva from other countries stayed only long enough to learn how to teach others and then went back, even if they had to face death.

Finally, in January 1559, Knox answered the call and went to Scotland, leaving Marjory and her mother behind. He stopped in Dieppe, on the coast of France, where he waited for a permit to land in England because sailing to England and then moving to Scotland was much safer than sailing to Scotland directly. While he was waiting, he agreed to preach for the Protestants in Dieppe, who didn't have a pastor. They had to meet secretly because France was a Roman Catholic country.

BACKGROUND: A BEACH AT DIEPPE. ©PAUL MAGNER

Soon, he was surprised to receive a message from the English royal court explaining that he could not pass through their country. The problem was a short book he had written in Geneva that said women should not rule a country. He had composed it as a message to some people in England, writing mainly about Mary Tudor, but a publisher had printed it for all to see.

This book, called *The First Blast of the Trumpet*, caused a lot of problems because, soon after it was published, a Protestant ruler—a woman— came to the throne of England: Elizabeth I. Even if Knox was willing to say that Elizabeth was an exception because of her faith, she was still furious and refused to let him enter her country. Knox finally admitted, "My *First Blast* has blown from me all my friends in England." It was a sad situation, but a few of his English friends remained close to him.

Queen Elizabeth I

CHAPTER SIX

The Scottish Revolution

Mary of Guise

eanwhile, the Christians in Dieppe received their French pastor, so in May 1559 Knox sailed directly to Scotland and landed at Leith, Edinburgh's port. Soon he realized he had arrived at a critical time. Mary of Guise was then ruling for her daughter, Mary Stuart, who had been living in the French royal court since she was six and was promised in marriage to young Francis, the future king of France.

At first Mary of Guise tried to keep peace with the large number of Protestants who lived in her country. By the time Knox arrived, however, she had enforced strong restrictions, forbidding them to preach or teach unless they were approved by the Catholic bishops. On the other hand, the Protestants were getting more numerous and demanded the right to worship according to their faith. The situation was tense. "The battle shall be great," Knox wrote to a friend. By this time, Knox and most of the Scottish lords had come to believe that when rulers ask their subjects to disobey God's Word, Christians not only can, but must rebel.

Knox started to preach immediately after his arrival. His sermons caused great excitement. One person said that he was "able, in one hour, to put more life in us than five hundred trumpets continually blustering in our ears."

In May, after he preached a fiery sermon explaining that making images of Jesus, God, and saints and praying to them is against the Bible, his listeners became so energized that they started to destroy all the pictures and statues in the church. The same thing happened in other cities. Soon there was an actual war, and Mary of Guise had to ask France to send more troops to help her. Seeing they could easily be outnumbered, the Protestant lords asked England to come to their rescue.

St. John's Church, where John Knox's fiery sermon started an uproar.

KILNBURN, WIKIMEDIA COMMONS

During this time, Knox became minister at St. Andrews, just as he had predicted on the galley. He kept busy not only as a preacher but also as a secretary and army chaplain. That meant he followed the troops to war to assist them and pray for them.

He found the struggle very tiring. He had not expected to face so many battles. "One day of troubles since my last arrival in Scotland has pierced my heart more than all the torments of the galleys in nineteen months," he wrote in a letter to a friend, "because that torment, for the most part, touched the body, but this one pierces the soul and the feelings."

While the English took their time to send reinforcements, the French army arrived and took over Edinburgh, sending away all the Protestant lords in the middle of the night. Knox called it a "dark and dolorous night" when the lords left "with shame and fear." Soon after that, he was able to preach a sermon of encouragement, inspiring God's people to continue to trust in Him.

Knox's sermons inspired God's people to continue to trust in Him.

Finally, in March 1560, the English army came to the rescue and defeated the French in battle. The French government tried to send 4,500 more men, but winter storms drove them back to France. After that, the French rulers became busy with problems at home, and in June Mary of Guise died.

At that point, everyone came to an agreement. France and England agreed to take their troops out of Scotland, and Mary Stuart allowed the Scottish lords to form a new parliament (a group of people with the power to make laws). By that time, she had married Francis, who had become King Francis II. As queen consort of France, she had no plans to return to her home country.

JOHN HAWES

Magdalen Chapel,
where the first General Assembly of
the Scottish church met in 1560.

In those days, the government of a country worked together with the church. One of the first decisions of the new Scottish Parliament was that Scotland was going to be a Protestant country. Knox and five other preachers, all named John, were invited to write a confession of faith for the new Scottish church. Confessions of faith are important because they help people understand what a church believes, and they recognize the main teachings of the Bible.

The Scots Confession of Faith is one of the first of these documents in Europe. It starts by describing God's story of salvation, from the creation of the world to the time Jesus went back to heaven, and helps us understand what this story means to us. It also explains how to recognize a true church: it must preach God's Word, perform the two sacraments instituted by Christ (baptism and the Lord's Supper), and help Christians in their fight against sin. It's easy to see that it was written by people who studied, preached, and loved God's Word because the language sounds very scriptural and straight from the heart. We can also see that it was written after a long struggle, because it reminds readers over and over of the constant fight between the church and the devil.

The confession was composed in only four days. On August 17, 1560, it was read twice, article by article, before Parliament. The majority approved it, and the Protestant ministers declared they were ready to defend the truth it proclaimed.

Besides the confession, the six Johns wrote a book called First Book of Discipline that set some rules for the church and the country. Some of the rules were meant to help the poor. The book also suggested there should be a school next to every church. When the Scottish Reformation started, only half the people living in cities could even write their names, and things were even worse in the country. The Reformers wanted to make sure that everyone could read the Bible. Because of this, the school system in Scotland became one of the best in Europe for some time. Often children had to read the Bible to their parents because the older generation had not gone to school.

Knox and five other men wrote the Scots Confession of Faith in four days.

DAVID ROSS

Knox's house in Edinburgh

In the meantime, Marjory, her mother, and the children had reunited with Knox, and they spent some happy days together. As leading preacher in Edinburgh, Knox lived in a comfortable house with a good salary. Their joy, however, didn't last long. Only a few months after her arrival, Marjory became sick and died. Calvin wrote Knox to express his sorrow at that difficult time. "You found a wife whose like is not found everywhere," he said. At the same time, Calvin was sure Knox could find true comfort in Christ. Because of this, he added, "I doubt not that you bear this calamity with patience."

Mrs. Bowes continued to live with Knox for a while, helping him to care for his sons. Three years later, she took them with her to England, where she made sure they attended a good school and college.

CHAPTER SEVEN
Facing the Queen

On August 19, 1561, Queen Mary Stuart returned to Scotland for the first time after thirteen years. Her husband had died suddenly from a serious infection, and French laws didn't allow her to continue as queen consort of France. In Scotland, she had to learn to rule over a Protestant country. Life there was very different from what she had known.

Mary Stuart,
Queen of the Scots

Some Scottish lords were willing to allow Mary to keep her Roman Catholic worship (called mass) in the privacy of her palace, but Knox was shocked by the idea. Like the other Protestant Reformers, he believed the mass was an act of idolatry and a great offense to God. He explained: "All worshiping, honoring, or service invented by the brain of man in the religion of God, without his own express commandment, is idolatry. The mass is invented by the brain of man, without any commandment of God; therefore it is idolatry." At the end of a sermon, he said, "One mass is more fearful to me, than if ten thousand armed enemies were landed in any part of the realm."

Obviously, Mary was not pleased to hear this, and she asked Knox to explain what he thought was true religion and if subjects should obey rulers in all things. Knox explained that only God in His Word—not rulers—can tell people how to worship Him properly. In other things people should obey their rulers unless they are asked to disobey God. If rulers start killing people who are trying to obey God, the subjects should send the rulers to prison, just like a son should stop a father who has become violent because of mental illness.

When she heard this, Mary looked amazed and didn't speak for fifteen minutes. No one had ever talked to her that way. After that, the two continued to discuss matters of religion. Even though they never agreed, the meeting ended peaceably, with Knox praying that God might bless the queen as He blessed Deborah in the Bible, if that was His will.

Knox met Mary three more times. At one point, she even asked Knox to become one of her advisors, but he refused. Maybe he thought she wanted to control what he was preaching. Each time they met, he told the queen very clearly what he thought God expected of her.

At Knox's words, Mary didn't speak for fifteen minutes.

The last of their meetings, in 1563, was not as peaceful. Mary had been looking for a new husband and was thinking of marrying the son of the king of Spain, who was heir to the throne and loyal to the Church of Rome. Knox saw the marriage as a great danger and encouraged the people to oppose it. Mary was furious. She asked Knox why her marriage was any of his business. In fact, she was so offended that she started to cry. Knox told her that he never enjoyed seeing others cry. He even hated to correct his children because he was always moved by their tears. At the same time, as a Scot, he was concerned about his country, and as a preacher, he believed it was his duty to warn others of danger.

Still upset, Mary tried to charge Knox with treason, but her councillors found him innocent, and she could not legally punish him. In spite of his victory, this was a difficult time for Knox. Many noblemen thought he was being too hard on the queen. Because of his strong convictions, he lost even some of his best friends.

The following year, Knox found some comfort in a new wife, the young Margaret Stewart, a distant relative of Queen Mary Stuart. Together, Knox and Margaret had three daughters: Martha, Margaret, and Elizabeth. Like Marjory, Margaret helped Knox with his paperwork and took care of him, especially as his health started to fail.

In the meantime, since Mary's plan to marry the Spanish nobleman failed, she set her heart on one of her cousins, Lord Darnley, who was eighteen years old—two years younger than she. Most people in Scotland didn't think Darnley would make a good king because he was arrogant and liked to spend his time drinking and having fun. When Mary married him anyway, she lost many supporters.

FROM AN ENGRAVING IN EDMUND LODGE, *PORTRAITS OF ILLUSTRIOUS PERSONAGES OF GREAT BRITAIN*, 1835

Henry Stuart, Lord Darnley

The marriage caused other serious problems. When Mary realized that her husband was not able to perform his royal duties, she started to rely more on her secretary, the Italian David Rizzio, and spent lots of time with him. Darnley became jealous and killed Rizzio right before her eyes. Eleven months later, Darnley was found dead in a building outside Edinburgh. People were horrified, but things became even worse when, two months later, Mary married the probable murderer, the Earl of Bothwell.

At this point, Mary lost even more supporters. The country came to the brink of a civil war as an army met Mary, Bothwell, and their forces in an open field, but, by evening, it was clear that her cause was lost. Mary was then imprisoned, and the Scottish nobles forced her to resign the crown. Next, her young son James, who was just a little more than one year old, was crowned King James VI of Scotland. Knox preached at his coronation.

James VI, king of Scotland
(James I of England)

OLD EDINBURGH IMAGES, ACTUAL EDUCATION LTD.

GRAEME ECCLES

A peaceful scene in the Ayrshire region, where Knox spent some time around the end of his life.

The queen's imprisonment caused a great division in the country, as she still had a few loyal followers eager to put her back on the throne. This situation was very discouraging for Knox, who had hoped for a more complete reformation of Scotland.

Knox had avoided most of the trouble during the last part of Mary's reign by traveling to England to visit his friends and his sons and by spending some time in the quiet region of Ayrshire, where he had many supporters and where he completed his book on the history of the Reformation in Scotland. This book is still considered one of the best sources of information on that period.

Eventually, Knox returned to Edinburgh, which continued to be a dangerous place. A historian who lived around that time tells us that someone tried to kill Knox by shooting a bullet through his window. The killer knew that Knox usually sat at the table with his back to the street. That day, however, Knox had decided to sit at the side, so the bullet passed over the empty chair and hit the bottom of a candlestick.

In spite of these challenges, Knox continued to preach, even while his body continued to become older and weaker. In fact, he seemed to find new energy every time he stood in the pulpit. In 1571, when he preached in St. Andrews, a university student explained that Knox had to be "lifted up to the pulpit," but once he was there he became so full of life that it looked like he wanted "to beat the pulpit to pieces and fly out of it."

Someone tried to kill Knox by shooting him.
The bullet came through his window and hit the bottom of a candlestick.

KIM TRAYNOR, WIKIMEDIA COMMONS

Statue of John Knox,
New College, Edinburgh, Scotland

Knox preached for the last time on November 9, 1572, and died of pneumonia fifteen days later. In the last days of his life, he asked his wife to read to him his favorite chapters from the Bible, especially John 17, the prayer Jesus said just before His death for those the Father had given Him.

After Knox's death, a nobleman said of him, "Here lies a man who in his life never feared nor flattered any man: who has been often threatened with pistol and dagger, but has ended his days in peace and honor."

In the last days of his life, Knox asked his wife to read to him his favorite chapters from the Bible.

Some people think Knox was a harsh and serious man because his words from the pulpit and in his writings were often strong. On the other hand, we know that many people loved him dearly as a pastor and friend. He was ready to admit that his way of speaking was not always pleasant. "By nature I am churlish [unrefined and difficult to work with]," he said. That's why he was very thankful for his friends. "I need them all more than any needs me," he added.

Near the end of his life, Knox was discouraged because his dream of bringing to Scotland the purity and simplicity of the church he had seen and led in Geneva seemed unreachable. There was so much disunity and violence in his country that he often thought of leaving. Still, God has continued to preserve the Scottish church, even through very difficult times.

In that church, Knox played an important role, energizing it with his passion and trying to keep it faithful to the Scriptures. Over time, his influence, as that of other Scottish Reformers, reached beyond the small boundaries of their country. Their insistence on the purity and simplicity of biblical worship has inspired other believers. Their vision for the organization of the church has become a model for many churches all over the world. Also, Christians who have faced political oppression have often turned to Knox's teachings to help them decide if it was time for them to submit to their rulers or stand up for what they believed was right.

Time Line of John Knox's Life

1514 – Knox is born in Haddington, Scotland.

1528 – Patrick Hamilton is the first Scot to be executed for his faith.

1542 – King James V dies. The newborn Mary Stuart becomes queen of Scotland.

1545 – Knox follows George Wishart.

1546 – Cardinal Beaton is murdered. Protestants take over St. Andrews Castle.

1547 – Knox moves to the castle. He preaches his first Protestant sermon. The castle is conquered, and Knox is imprisoned as a galley slave for nineteen months.

1549 – Knox becomes a pastor in Berwick, England.

1550 – He meets Mrs. Elizabeth Bowes and her daughter, Marjory.

1552 – He moves to London to be one of the king's preachers.

1553 – He is forced into hiding when Roman Catholic Mary Tudor becomes queen.

1554 – He flees to France, then Zurich and Geneva, Switzerland. He works for a short time as pastor of an English congregation in Frankfurt, Germany.

1555 – He goes back to Geneva. He returns to Scotland for a short time and marries Marjory Bowes.

1556 – He returns to Geneva with his wife and mother-in-law.

1558 – Elizabeth I becomes queen of England.

1559 – Knox returns to Scotland. His sermon against idolatry leads to a rebellion.

1560 – Mary of Guise dies. A Protestant parliament is established. Knox becomes pastor in Edinburgh. Marjory dies.

1561 – Mary Stuart returns to Scotland.

1564 – Knox marries Margaret Stewart.

1567 – Mary Stuart is forced to give up her crown, and her son, James, becomes king in her place. Knox preaches at his coronation.

1572 – Knox dies of pneumonia.

Did you know?

John Knox was not very tall. In fact, it seems that he was shorter than average. Someone said that he looked serious but not harsh. His eyes were dark blue and lively. He had a long face with a long nose and large lips.

Knox was buried in a churchyard outside St. Giles in Edinburgh. In the seventeenth century, the Scottish Parliament erected a new building and paved over the area, which is now the parking lot for the judges and advocates of the law courts next to Parliament House. Knox is probably buried under parking stall 23—though the courts change the number of their parking stalls from time to time, and a few years ago it was stall 16.

Sports were popular in John Knox's day, even if only the rich had time to devote to them. Queen Mary Stuart was almost six feet tall and athletic. She liked riding horses, hunting, archery, tennis, and golf. In fact, she loved golf so much that she played with friends just days after her husband, Lord Darnley, was killed and caused much disapproval. She is said to be the first woman golfer in Scotland. She also liked to watch football (soccer). When Elizabeth imprisoned her in the Castle of Carlisle, England, she was allowed twice to cheer her male servants in a game of football.

The First Book of Discipline explained how each church should be organized, with one or more pastors, some elders, and deacons. The pastors and elders formed a group known as the kirk session (kirk is the Scottish word for church). This type of church was later called Presbyterian, from the Greek word *presbyter*, which means "elder." In Knox's time, church sessions met at least once a week. People went to see the session for any type of problem and also for happy announcements, such as a decision to get married.

The Reformers took every image and statue out of church buildings. No more candles or incense burned, no longer did the priests and bishops wear fancy and colorful gowns, and organs were no longer played. There was not much to see or smell, but there was a lot of God's Word to read and hear. The pastor read and preached the Bible, everyone sang the Psalms, children memorized the catechism, and families reviewed the sermon together after each service.

The Reformation in Scotland changed the way people spent their Sundays. Instead of attending one brief Roman Catholic worship service, people went to two services a day, one in the morning and one in the afternoon, with sermons that lasted much longer than they did in the Roman Catholic Church. Between the services, someone taught the catechism. The second service started in the early afternoon so people could get back home before dark. To stay on schedule, the session allowed preachers only about one hour for their sermons. They had an hour glass to keep time, and sometimes preachers who spoke too long were fined.

Before the Reformation, the music in the church was elaborate; the words of the songs, usually psalms, were in Latin, and they were performed by a choir. During the Reformation, all the people sang psalms in their own language. This helped most people memorize them. Singing was also used (but not during church services) to memorize the catechism, Lord's Prayer, and Ten Commandments.

✿ In Protestant Scotland, going to church on Sunday was required by law. People could stay home if they were sick or had to do some necessary work, such as taking care of someone in need. Those who skipped church without a good reason were fined. To the Reformers, skipping church was as bad as breaking any other law because they believed that God blessed the preaching of the gospel to save people and to move them to holy living.

Mandatory church attendance had its challenges. Some people misbehaved in church because they didn't want to be there. Also, often the buildings were so crowded that people had no room to move. One church had to build portable Communion tables that hung on the walls to make more room for people to sit.

✿ Mary Stuart had a huge wardrobe that included gowns made of silver or gold cloth, silk, satin, velvet, or damask; petticoats and chemises (both underdresses); silk stockings; and farthingales (support hoops to hold up the underskirts). She also had many pairs of velvet shoes laced with silver and gold, dozens of hats, many pairs of perfumed gloves, and thirty-three costumes for masquerade parties.

She liked to dress up, and not just for masquerades. As many rulers in her day, sometimes she disguised herself as a common person to mingle with her people and understand what they thought. Once she even dressed up as a man. In Lochleven, she made two attempts to escape prison by dressing as a servant. The first time, however, she was discovered when the boatman noticed her lily-white hands.

When she finally fled to England, she left all her belongings behind and took only what she was wearing and could carry. She finally managed to get some supplies from France, but during her imprisonment she chose to wear only black, because she felt that it suited her circumstances better.

Her favorite color, however, was white. At her first wedding, she shocked everyone by wearing a fully white gown. In France, queens wore white only after someone had died. The usual colors for royal wedding gowns were gold, silver, or purple.

The Stewarts were a famous family in Scotland. Mary, however, changed the spelling of the name to "Stuart" when she was in France to make sure people could pronounce it correctly. This is why Knox's second wife, who was a distant relative to Queen Mary, spelled her last name differently from Mary.

After ten months of imprisonment in Lochleven Castle, Mary Stuart escaped, fled to England, and begged Queen Elizabeth: "Have compassion on my great misfortunes and permit me to come to you." She wanted to ask Elizabeth to give her an army to put her back on the Scottish throne. Instead, Elizabeth held her prisoner for nineteen years. Elizabeth feared Mary because she was a relative of King Henry VIII and had a claim to the English throne. Finally, in 1586, Mary became involved in a plot to kill Elizabeth, who then had her executed as a traitor.

In 1603, after Elizabeth's death, King James VI of Scotland inherited the throne of England as King James I. As a result, the crowns were united, and James ruled over both countries, even though each country retained its own parliament. The British flag, with the red cross of England in front and the white cross of Scotland on a blue background in the back, first appeared then. In 1707, the two parliaments combined, and the two countries became known as Great Britain.

In 1604, King James authorized a new version of the English Bible (known as the King James Version), which is still used by many Christians today.

The Scots Confession of Faith

CHAPTERS 1–4

Chapter 1—God

We confess and acknowledge one God alone, to whom alone we must cleave, whom alone we must serve, whom only we must worship, and in whom alone we put our trust. Who is eternal, infinite, immeasurable, incomprehensible, omnipotent, invisible; one in substance and yet distinct in three persons, the Father, the Son, and the Holy Ghost. By whom we confess and believe all things in heaven and earth, visible and invisible to have been created, to be retained in their being, and to be ruled and guided by His inscrutable providence for such end as His eternal wisdom, goodness, and justice have appointed, and to the manifestation of His own glory.

Chapter 2—The Creation of Man

We confess and acknowledge that our God has created man, i.e., our first father, Adam, after His own image and likeness, to whom He gave wisdom, lordship, justice, free will, and self-consciousness, so that in the whole nature of man no imperfection could be found. From this dignity and perfection man and woman both fell; the woman being deceived by the serpent and man obeying the voice of the woman, both conspiring against the sovereign majesty of God, who in clear words had previously threatened death if they presumed to eat of the forbidden tree.

Chapter 3—Original Sin

By this transgression, generally known as original sin, the image of God was utterly defaced in man, and he and his children became by nature hostile to God, slaves to Satan, and servants to sin. And thus everlasting death has had, and shall have, power and dominion over all who have not been, are not, or shall not be born from above. This rebirth is wrought by the power of the Holy Ghost creating in the hearts of God's chosen ones an assured faith in the promise of God revealed to us in His Word; by this faith we grasp Christ Jesus with the graces and blessings promised in Him.

> You can ask your parents to help you find the complete Scots Confession online or in a library and read it together.

Chapter 4—The Revelation of the Promise

We constantly believe that God, after the fearful and horrible departure of man from His obedience, did seek Adam again, call upon him, rebuke and convict him of his sin, and in the end made unto him a most joyful promise, that "the seed of the woman should bruise the head of the serpent," that is, that He should destroy the works of the devil. This promise was repeated and made clearer from time to time; it was embraced with joy, and most constantly received by all the faithful from Adam to Noah, from Noah to Abraham, from Abraham to David, and so onwards to the incarnation of Christ Jesus; all (we mean the believing fathers under the law) did see the joyful day of Christ Jesus, and did rejoice.

Acknowledgments

I don't know if my young readers take the time to read the acknowledgments, but the long list of people who are making these books possible tells an exciting story of God's providence and provision and is an encouraging and touching example of kindness, generosity, and love for truthfulness and beauty.

For this book, I want to especially thank Dr. Rosalind K. Marshall, fellow of the Royal Society of Literature and author of *John Knox* (among many other books on Scottish history); Jane Dawson, professor of Reformation history at The University of Edinburgh, currently working on a major biography of John Knox for Yale University Press; Suzanne McDonald, assistant professor of religion at Calvin College and author of *John Knox for Armchair Theologians*; Forrest Howie, company director at Historic Edinburgh Tours Actual Education; Philip Benedict, professor at the University of Geneva's Institute for Reformation History; and Ewen A. Cameron, professor of Scottish history and paleography at the University of Edinburgh, who have taken time from their studies, research, writing, and teaching to either read my manuscript or answer my many questions—or both.

Other people who have read the manuscript of this book include my friends Heather Chisholm-Chait and Dianna Ippolito; Westminster Seminary of California students Tim Massaro and Brenden Link; my children Kevin, Raphael, and Renaissance; and my Sunday school students Isaiah Brindis De Salas, Hannah Erikson, and James, Matthew, Olivia, and Adam Horton. I couldn't have done without their valuable insights. And I must say that the excitement I saw in the eyes of my students was the best encouragement I have received with this project.

I am very touched by all the people who have provided photos free of charge or for a minimal fee. This is very rare today, and I will always be deeply grateful for their generosity. Please look at their names by each photo.

I am also thankful for Tom Carroll, who faithfully continues to draw maps for these books; for my outstanding illustrator, Matt Abraxas; and for the support of my husband, Tom, and my church family at Christ United Reformed Church.

I wish my young readers could also know how much help, advice, and support I have received from Dr. Joel Beeke, Jay Collier, Steve Renkema, Annette Gysen, David Woollin, and the other staff at Reformation Heritage Books. They are the ones ultimately responsible for the quality and accuracy of these books, and their commitment and hard work is evident in the end products.